PROCRASTINATION

Understanding, signs, types, and tips to avoid being caught up in this act And the new life activities to stay active

James BLESSINGS

TABLE OF CONTENT

CHAPTER 1

WHAT IS PROCRASTINATION, WHY DO PEOPLE PROCRASTINATE

Stalling is one of the primary obstructions hindering you from getting up, pursuing the ideal choices, and carrying on with the fantasy life you've considered.

Late investigations have shown that individuals lament more the things they haven't done than the things they have done. Moreover, sensations of disappointment and culpability coming about because of botched open doors will generally remain with individuals significantly longer.

Here and there the entirety of our chances appear to be readily available, yet we just can't contact them. At the point when you dawdle, you sit around that you could be putting resources into something significant. If you can defeat this furious adversary, you will want to achieve more and in improving use the potential that life brings to the table.

For what reason DO PEOPLE PROCRASTINATE?

Resolution is frequently seen to be the main source of hesitation, yet predominantly our inborn inspiration assists us with conquering the propensity for putting things off on a consistent schedule.

Choice

The quantity of chances that the present world offers is faltering. Present-day culture venerates individual freedom in the conviction that the more liberated individuals are, the more joyful they will be. So why aren't individuals today fundamentally more joyful than previously? Since with more opportunities to pursue our own choices and to play out our activities, we have become effortlessly befuddled about what is fundamentally important, what is fundamental and what isn't, and what is good and bad, and thusly we have become demotivated to do anything by any stretch of the imagination.

We want to sort out our qualities and individual dreams and develop positive propensities. This is the fundamental thing that can assist us with conquering lingering as well as the wide range of various snags that life brings.

Overlooking The Value of Time

We were completely conceived and sadly sooner or later will all kick the bucket as well. The time we spend on Earth is both restricted and limited. Considering these realities, time is the most significant product you have. It's not cash; dissimilar to time, you can acquire cash, save, or procure more. You can't do that with time. Every subsequent you squander is gone for eternity.

The simple acknowledgment that life is limited leads individuals to start dealing with their time all the more cautiously. It makes you ponder how you might preferably want to invest your energy on Earth.

Absence of self-restraint

You can envision self-restraint or poise as a second when you provide yourself orders, however, you are struggling with following them. It isn't the essential driver of hesitation yet at the same a significant compound. To be focused, you want to have the right kind of inspiration and figure out how to keep up with and work on sure propensities.

Kinds of inspiration and why laying out objectives won't ever work

Outward inspiration

Prizes and disciplines or incentives were formed to compel individuals into performing activities they could never consider all alone. Be that as it may, when individuals do things they would rather not do, they are less blissful, and their cerebrums discharge less dopamine. Many examinations have affirmed that involving extraneous inspiration brings down execution in exercises that require even a little brainwork and imagination.

Extraneous inspiration

Objective based inspiration

This inspiration drives individuals forward, making them buckle down for their objectives, and that implies that eventually, they will to be sure accomplish them. Furthermore, when that at long last occurs, a one-time portion of dopamine is delivered, bringing about an extreme feeling of happiness. The issue that follows next is a peculiarity known as decadent transformation. This makes individuals get acquainted with their cultivated objectives suddenly. A couple of moments, hours, or, probably, days after arriving at an objective, good sentiments will vanish.

Objective based inspiration

Inherent inspiration

Significance and vision give enduring and fulfilling inspiration. At the point when individuals see the reason in their activities, especially when they need to play out these activities, one of the most grounded types of inspiration emerges, it is called natural excursion-based inspiration. This sort of inspiration depends on the idea of having an individual vision. Not at all like pursuing objectives, an individual vision is a declaration of something enduring. It responds to the subject of how you might most want to invest your energy throughout everyday life. It centers around activities, not results. It centers around the excursion, not the objective.

CHAPTER 2

Indications OF PROCRASTINATION
Holding on as late as possible before cutoff times to get everything rolling.

Ending up performing undertakings that you planned to do days prior.

Constantly saying "I'll do it later" (or something almost identical, to "I'll do it tomorrow").

Stalling out in impartial even though you know that it is so vital to get everything rolling.

Unnecessarily postponing getting done with responsibilities, regardless of whether they're significant.

Deferring dealing with things you could do without doing.

Promising yourself you'll follow through with something and then stalling as opposed to making it happen.

Deferring beginning undertakings that look unappealing (e.g., exhausting, baffling, or hard).

Requires days to get done with even tasks that require little else aside from plunking down and doing them.

Continuously having pardons for not getting things done on time.

Continually investing further develops your effort propensities.

Putting off deciding.

Attempting to begin regardless of whether you disdain yourself for it.

The greater amount of these signs and side effects you show, and the more truly you do as such, the more
possible it is that you're a slacker,

CHAPTER 3

.Kinds OF PROCRASTINATION

1. According to the entertainer, "I function admirably under tension"

These slackers compel themselves to concentrate by contracting the time they need to handle an errand. For the overwhelming majority of our clients, the genuine purpose for this is compulsiveness. Assuming that you're tight on time, its assignment should be possible to your absurdly elevated requirements in any case, correct? For other people, the issue is falling once again into old examples and convictions that we have about our last-minute recoveries. Regardless of anything, being prone to come down on yourself isn't practical.

Getting everything rolling.
Switch things up and set a beginning date. At the point when you center around while you will start an errand and not when you desire to end it you'll take an enormous measure of tension off of yourself.

2. The self-deprecator who says, "I am so sluggish at this moment"
This slacker is something contrary to apathetic, so when they don't accomplish something they are extra unforgiving with themselves. We see this a ton with our male clients. They will generally pin inaction on sluggishness or hardheadedness as opposed to conceding they are worn out. What they need is to be more sympathetic with themselves.

Enjoy some time off. We realize you will say you lack the opportunity and energy to rest.

: Re-energize. Go for a stroll to give yourself space and start revamping your energy.

3. The overbooker who says, "I'm so occupied"
This slowpoke is a genius at topping off their schedule and is frequently wrecked. "I'm so occupied" is presumably the reason we hear most frequently. Curiously, probably the most active individuals we work with finish the most. At the point when hecticness comes up as a reason for not following through with something, it's generally a sign of aversion. As opposed to dealing with a test directly or conceding, that they would rather not follow through with something, it's simpler to find fault with having other significant activities.

Making mayhem to try not to confront what you realize you want to confront at present

Pause for a minute of contemplation. Ask yourself: What am I keeping away from?

4. According to the oddity searcher, "I just had the smartest thought!"
This slacker has a terminal instance of Shiny Object Syndrome. They're continually concocting new ventures to take on and afterward getting exhausted with them seven days after the fact. They're captivated by the most recent pattern and will rush to execute yet not see everything through to completion.

They are perfect at simply deciding and making a move. Nonetheless, they end up unintentionally losing a great deal of time and wearing out because they don't steer reliable activity in one course to the point of getting results. A large number of our pioneering clients fit into this classification

CHAPTER 4

Impacts OF PROCRASTINATION

The adverse consequences of lingering can go from basically missing a cutoff time on a significant errand to something all the more long haul, like a botched open door that kills a fantasy. A few of us may be sufficiently fortunate to recognize our propensity to linger in time regardless take care of business.

For other people, it can have enduring impacts that reverberate all through their lives.

The explanation we delay differs from one individual to another and isn't clear 100% of the time. In some cases, it is a secret trepidation that we would rather not recognize, or it really might be as straightforward as not having any desire to accomplish something since it simply doesn't persuade us.

Anything that the explanation might be, on the off chance that you realize you are a slowpoke, you ought to be cautious, as it has undeniably more harming impacts than you might understand. You can see whether you're an ongoing slowpoke with this free evaluation: Are You a Chronic Procrastinator?

Here are the 8 most normal impacts of stalling that can annihilate your efficiency as well as your life.

1. Losing Precious Time
How long have you squandered tarrying?

The most awful thing about stalling is the second you understand that you are two, five, or a decade more established and nothing has changed.

This is a horrendous inclination since you can't turn around the hands of time; you simply need to live with the powerless sensation of disappointment. There isn't anything more awful than feeling disappointed at yourself, realizing what is going on might have been so unique if by some stroke of good luck you had ventured out.

2. Blowing Opportunities

What number of chances have you squandered because you didn't make the most of them when they were there? This is the point at which the impacts of hesitation make you need to kick yourself.

What you don't understand is that the open door might have been life getting updated, yet you passed up it. Most open doors just come around once; you have rarely ensured another opportunity.

Valuable open doors are the world's approach to giving you more, so help yourself out and get them with two hands when they introduce themselves.

3. Not Meeting Goals
Hesitation appears to come on with full power when we consider objectives, of needing to accomplish or change something. You could want to change, yet you just apparently can't venture out forward.

This is typically befuddling and puzzling; you could wind up thinking, "For what reason is it so difficult to go for something that I need so seriously?" Only you can respond to that; you'll need to investigate somewhat more profound into the obstruction.

We put forth objectives since we truly want to better our lives here and there. If you don't do this due to lingering, you lessen the likelihood to better your life.

Reveal the underlying driver behind your hesitation if it's keeping you from accomplishing your objectives, or you might in all likelihood never achieve them.

4. Demolishing a Career
How you work straightforwardly influences your outcomes, the amount you accomplish, and how well you perform, so the impacts of delaying can turn out to be unfavorable to your vocation.

Lingering might keep you from complying with time constraints or accomplishing your month-to-month targets. What outcome will this, at last, have on your vocation?

You could pass up advancements or even be in danger of losing your employment. You can attempt to conceal it for some time, however, don't question that drawn-out hesitation at work will more than likely ruin your vocation.

5. Lower Self-Esteem
This is one of the awful circles you could think of yourself as in. We will quite often hesitate because low confidence causes us to feel that we will not have the option to finish an errand or task the correct way. Tragically, delaying just expands sensations of low confidence, making us question ourselves significantly more.

One review including 426 undergrads viewed that "scholarly hesitation was adversely anticipated by confidence and restraint

At the point when we have low confidence, we keep ourselves down, feel disgraceful of accomplishment, and start to behave destructively. Tarrying consumes your certainty, gradually.

On the off chance that this impacts you, center around building your confidence as opposed to clutching the deception that you ought to have the option to follow through with something, as this makes you drive yourself into something when you are not prepared.

6. Settling on Poor Choices

Unfortunate independent direction is one of the most awful impacts of tarrying. At the point when you stall, you settle on choices given models that most probably wouldn't be there on the off chance that you didn't hesitate, similar to strain to at long last choose because there's simply no time to spare.

Feelings vigorously impact the choices we make, and stalling increments pessimistic feelings, which can drive us into pursuing choices that don't serve us over the long haul.

Rather than racing through choices while tarrying, work out every one of the potential outcomes and track down a quiet second to investigate the advantages and disadvantages of each.

7. Harm to Your Reputation

At the point when you continue saying you will follow through with something and you don't, your standing gets discolored, as no one needs void commitments. Other than harming your standing, you are harming your confidence and fearlessness. You will find that it gets simpler to dawdle each time since you are not shocking yourself any longer.

Individuals could quit relying upon you and keep down on offering you potential open doors since they could be concerned that you will essentially delay, halting them to tidy up the wreck.

Regardless of whether you as of now have a standing of being a slowpoke, you can turn it around. Next time somebody asks you for something, utilize every one of the apparatuses available to you to make it happen on time. Each time you satisfy a solicitation, your standing will start to develop back, which will prompt more open doors and better associations with people around you.

8. Taking a chance with Your Health
Among the impacts of delaying are psychological well-being issues like pressure and tension, and these, thus, are connected to medical problems. Assuming your hesitation prompts sensations of despondency, this will begin to influence different parts of your life.

Assuming you stall a lot with something, it will no doubt begin to worry you and cause uneasiness, particularly when others or things are involved, and all of this, thusly, to chronic weakness results.
Another way that stalling can influence your wellbeing in the present moment is the

point at which you consistently put off check-ups and delay arrangements or things you want to do, like activity. The issue just deteriorates and the results are direr.

The impacts of dawdling may not appear to be all that terrible from the start, yet over the long haul, those impacts can construct, prompting pressure, nervousness, broken dreams, and low confidence. Rather than allowing dawdling to grab hold, carve out an opportunity to foster time usage strategies to assist you with managing it when it shows up.

In Interferon dawdling mediations, analysts found that mental social treatment essentially decreased lingering and "diminished delaying more emphatically than different sorts of mediations. On the off chance that you wind up proceeding to battle with dawdling, mental conduct treatment might be an extraordinary choice to attempt.

CHAPTER 5

KEYS TO AVOIDING PROCRASTINATION

Many individuals/understudies eventually in time and secondary school have procrastinated in beginning their schoolwork, finishing an undertaking, or reading up for a test. Delaying is likewise normal among understudies. You most likely understand what you ought to do however you simply don't have any desire to make it happen. It's not difficult to invest off hard or energy-consuming tasks as late as possible, yet if you do, you might need to pull pressure-prompted dusk 'til dawn affair. Here are a few hints to keep away from tarrying.

GET ORGANIZED

You are bound to stall if you don't have a set arrangement or thought for finishing your work. Putting resources into an organizer is smart. Begin monitoring every one of your tasks and their due dates. At the point when you're coordinated, it gives you a more systematic and estimated structure inside which to work.

Dispense with DISTRACTIONS

Disposing of interruptions is one more tip to stay away from delays. By restricting the number of interruptions around you, you're bound to finish what you want to do. Shut your telephone down, retreat to a calm spot and pay attention to traditional music or repetitive sound that overwhelm any commotion.

Focus on

Focusing on your work and tasks is one more method for assisting you with keeping away from hesitation. Consistently, make a rundown of what should be finished. Ensure you address the most basic or time-delicate tasks first. Then work your direction down the rundown. Move the hard stuff first, so all that comes after it will appear to be more sensible.

Put forth GOALS

Part of the explanation you could tarry is that what you need to do appears to be overpowering. It's much more straightforward to begin on a task when you lay out basic, reachable objectives as opposed to confronting a major, obscure arrangement. Rather than telling yourself, "I'll concentrate on science this evening," you could rather say, "I'll concentrate on part six this evening." This makes your objectives not so much scary but rather more feasible.

SET DEADLINES

One more tip to stay away from lingering is to set cutoff times. Numerous understudies stall out in the "I'll do it tomorrow or at last" cycle when in truth that day or ultimately never comes. It means quite a bit to set a particular date for when you maintain that a venture or task should be finished. Expect to have your undertakings and tasks finished a couple of days ahead of time. Like that, if something startling occurs, you have an additional chance to finish them.

Enjoy some time off

One more tip to stay away from delaying is to take a 10-to 15-minute break from your school or w sometimes. Pay attention to music, go for a stroll, or — anything that removes your psyche from your everyday schedule and permits you to unwind. enjoying some time off can increment center, lessen pressure, and assist you with better holding data.

REWARD YOURSELF

Compensating yourself might make a motivating force to get done with a job and assist with staying away from dawdling. In the wake of reading up for a test or finishing a task, think about compensating yourself. It very well may be pretty much as basic as, "When I finish this task, I can watch an episode of my #1 show."

Consider YOURSELF ACCOUNTABLE
Considering yourself responsible for finishing your tasks on time, reading up for tests, and getting passing marks isn't just a significant ability to survive in school, it's one more tip to stay away from delays. While it is not difficult to track down motivations not to study and enjoy superfluous or extra-extended reprieves, get yourself before this occurs. Recall that you are liable for the tasks you complete or don't finish, the tests you pro or don't excel on, and your grades. If you want assistance in considering yourself responsible, tell a companion or relative and request that they determine the status of your objectives, cutoff times, and achievements.

CHAPTER 6

Presently A NEW LIFE

1. Acknowledge that there is no 'wonderful' balance between fun and serious activities. At the point when you hear "balance between serious and fun activities," you most likely envision having an incredibly useful day at work and leaving right on time to enjoy the other portion of the day with loved ones. While this might appear to be great, it is absurd 100% of the time.

Try not to take a stab at the ideal timetable; take a stab at a sensible one. Every so often, you could zero in more on work, while on different days you could have additional significant investment to seek after your leisure activities or invest energy with your friends and family. Balance is accomplished over the long haul, not every day.

"It is vital to stay liquid and continually survey where you are [versus] your objectives and needs, "Now and again, your kids might require you, and at different times, you might have to go to work, yet permitting yourself to stay open to diverting and evaluating your necessities on any day is key in tracking down the balance."

2. Get a new line of work that you love. Even though work is a normal cultural standard, your profession ought not to be limiting. Assuming you disdain what you do, you won't be blissful, easy. You don't have to cherish each part of your work, however, it should be energizing enough that you don't fear getting up each day.

getting a new line of work that you are so energetic about you would do it free of charge. "Assuming your occupation is depleting you, and you are finding it hard to do the things you love beyond work, something is off-base, "You might be working in a harmful climate, for a poisonous individual, or finishing a work that you genuinely don't cherish. If so, the time has come to get another line of work."

3. Focus on your wellbeing.
Your generally speaking physical, close to home and emotional well-being ought to be your fundamental concern. Assuming you battle with nervousness or sadness and figure treatment would help you, fit those meetings into your timetable, regardless of whether you need to go home early or ditch your night turn class. If you are fighting a persistent disease, feel free to phone in wiped out on harsh days. Exhausting yourself keeps you from improving, perhaps making you go home for the days later.

Focusing on your wellbeing as a matter of some importance will make you a superior representative and individual, "You will miss less work, and when you are there, you will be more joyful and more useful."

Focusing on your wellbeing doesn't need to comprise of revolutionary or outrageous exercises. It very well may be pretty much as straightforward as day-to-day contemplation or exercise.

4. Don't hesitate for even a moment to turn it off.
Cutting binds with the rest of the world every once in a while permits us to recuperate from the week-after-week stress and gives us space for different contemplations and thoughts to arise. Turning off can mean something straightforward like rehearsing travel reflection on your day-to-day drive, rather than browsing work messages.

.

5. Getaway.
Some of the time, genuinely turning off implies taking downtime and closing work totally off for some time. Whether your get-away comprises of a one-day staycation

or a fourteen-day excursion to Bali, it's vital to require investment to genuinely and intellectually re-energize.

Representatives are in many cases stressed that getting some much-needed rest will disturb the work process, and they will be met with an excess of work when they return. This dread shouldn't limit you from having some long overdue time off.

"Truly, there is no respectability in not removing merited time from work; the advantages of going home for the day far offset the drawbacks, "With legitimate preparation, you can remove time without stressing over troubling your partners or battling with a tremendous responsibility when you return."

6. Set aside a few minutes for you as well as your friends and family.
While your occupation is significant, it ought not to be as long as you can

remember. You were a person before taking this position, and you ought to focus on the exercises or leisure activities that fulfill you. accomplishing a balance between fun and serious activities requires purposeful activity.

"On the off chance that you don't immovably make arrangements for individual time, you won't have the opportunity to do different things beyond work," No matter how rushed your timetable may be, you eventually have control of your time and life."

While arranging a time with your friends and family, make a schedule for heartfelt and family dates. It might appear to be peculiar to design one-on-one time with somebody you live with, yet it will guarantee that you invest quality energy with them without work-life struggle. Since work keeps you occupied doesn't mean you ought to disregard individual connections.

"Understand that nobody at your organization will cherish you or value you how your friends and family do," "Likewise [remember] that everybody is replaceable working, and regardless of how significant you think your occupation is, the organization won't overlook anything tomorrow assuming you are no more."

7. Put down stopping points and work hours.

Put down stopping points for you as well as your partners, to stay balanced. At the point when you leave the workplace, abstain from contemplating impending ventures or noting organization messages. Consider having a different PC or telephone for work, so you can shut it down when you call it a day. If that is unimaginable, utilize separate programs, messages, or channels for your work and individual stages.

Also, "Whether you work away from home or at home, it is critical to decide when you will work and when you will quit working; any other way, you could wind up noting business-related messages late around evening time, during excursions, or on ends of the week off,

advising colleagues and your chief about limits past which you can't be available because you are taking part in private exercises. This will assist with guaranteeing that they comprehend and regard your work cutoff points and assumptions.

8. Put forth objectives and boundaries (and stick to them).
Put forth attainable objectives by executing time-usage systems, examining your daily agenda, and removing errands that have practically no worth.

Focus on when you are generally useful working and block that downtime for your most significant business-related exercises. Try not to browse your messages and telephone at regular intervals, as those are significant time-squandering undertakings that wreck your consideration and efficiency. Organizing your day can increment efficiency at work, which can bring about more available energy to loosen up beyond work

www.ingramcontent.com/pod-product-compliance
Lightning Source LLC
LaVergne TN
LVHW020533160826
845677LV00015B/4034

9798351618548